SIMPLE EYES

& OTHER POEMS

D1431466

ALSO BY MICHAEL McCLURE

POETRY
Hymns to Saint Geryon
Dark Brown
The New Book / A Book of
    Torture
Ghost Tantras
Little Odes
Organism
Star
September Blackberries
Rare Angel
Jaguar Skies
Antechamber
Fragments of Perseus
Selected Poems
Rebel Lions

NOVELS
The Mad Cub
The Adept

PLAYS
The Blossom
The Mammals
The Beard
Gargoyle Cartoons
The Grabbing of the Fairy

Gorf
Josephine the Mouse Singer
VKTMS

ESSAYS
Meat Science Essays
Scratching the Beat Surface
Specks
Testa Coda
Lighting the Corners

COLLABORATIVE
"Mercedes Benz," with Janis
    Joplin
Mandala Book, with Bruce
    Conner
Freewheelin Frank, Secretary of
    the Angels: As Told to Michael
    McClure, by Frank Reynolds

C.D., VIDEO, AND
CASSETTE
Love Lion, video, with Ray
    Manzarek
Love Lion, C.D., with Ray
    Manzarek
Ghost Tantras, audio cassette,

SIMPLE
EYES

& OTHER POEMS

MICHAEL McCLURE

A NEW DIRECTIONS BOOK

Some of these poems have appeared in *Angel Island, Café Solo, Citivoice, City, Conjunctions, Cover, Exquisite Corpse, Howl, New York Quarterly, Off the Wall, Poetry U.S.A., San Jose Studies, Shambala Sun, Talisman,* and some had their first appearance at music clubs like the Bottom Line and The Great American Music Hall in concert with Ray Manzarek playing the piano. Jerry Reddan's Tangram Press published a limited, fine press edition, *What Crevices,* which included six poems from the "Black Rows" section of this book. "Red Cages" and "Boulder Hill" originally appeared in a pamphlet, *Red Cages,* from Mel Thompson's Blue Beetle Press.

Designed by Amy Evans
Manufactured in the United States of America
New Directions Book are printed on acid-free paper.
First published as New Directions Paperbook 780 in 1994
Published simultaneously in Canada by Penguin Books Canada Limited

LIBRARY OF CONGRESS CATALOGING IN PUBLICATION DATA
McClure, Michael.
    Simple eyes & other poems / Michael McClure.
      p.   cm. — (New Directions paperbook; 780)
    ISBN 0-8112-1265-3
    I. Title. II. Title: Simple eyes and other poems.
PS3563.A262S5 1994
811'.54—dc20   93-46673
                          CIP

New Directions Books are published for James Laughlin
by New Directions Publishing Corporation,
80 Eighth Avenue, New York 10011

CONTENTS

vii Author's Introduction

SPIRIT'S DESPERADO

3 Spirit's Desperado
4 Cream Hidden
5 The Last Waltz
6 Old Warhols
7 Writing to You from Seattle

MEXICAN MOUNTAINS

11 Mexico Seen from the Moving Car
13 The Butterfly
14 Quetzalcoatl Song
16 Reading Frank O'Hara in a Mexican Rainstorm
17 Mirroring Flame in the Fireplace

SIMPLE EYES

20 Foreword
22 Fields 1–9
40 A
42 B
44 Fields 10–13
52 The Foam

BLACK ROWS

59 Grieved Skull
63 Edge Chunk
77 Summer Hummingbird
78 Hotel Santa Monica

81 Haiku of the Hunt

82 Brain Damage—Lies!

84 Gorgeousness

86 To Robert Creeley (One)

88 To Robert Creeley (Two)

90 Haikus

91 Through the Bars

92 Spontaneous Poem Beginning with Lines from
      the Tao Te Ching

94 Senate Hearings

CHRISTMAS IN KENYA

97 The Cheetah

99 Old Eyes

101 Near Mount Kenya

103 Thoughts on Travel and Art

105 At Noon by the Red-Brown River

107 Christmas Morning in Samburu

108 Leaving the Fairview Hotel

MOMENT'S MUSE

111 American Dream

113 Cowboy

115 Moment's Muse

118 Red Cages

125 Boulder Hill

129 Notes

AUTHOR'S INTRODUCTION

Emily Dickinson speaks of the myriad-mindedness that one finds on getting deeper into consciousness; she says, "Split the Lark—and you'll find the Music—Bulb after Bulb, in Silver rolled..." When my Lark of poetry is split I find that I've written a poem titled "Spirit's Desperado." Many of us who began to write in the fifties were desperados, and in the teeth of the times we were outlaws. But now anyone with deep human or humane feelings is something like an outlaw.

Another surprise in *Simple Eyes* is to find that I have written a poem about Warhol's art, which was once shocking to some, but now how pastoral it looks among present brutalities.

It should not have been a surprise that I returned again to the concept of *agnosia,* to the idea of knowing through not-knowing, and have written a new poem, "Edge Chunk," as blindly as mystics of the fourteenth century looked out with their deliberately sightless consciousnesses. "Edge Chunk" has a blues sound when I perform it at music clubs with keyboardist Ray Manzarek. It is dedicated to the bluesman Willie Dixon; it could have also been dedicated to Thelonious Monk or to the early seeker through *agnosia,* Dionysius the Areopagite.

I had a plan to write stanzas about the Gulf War and have them bloom out of images and photos of myself in the wars I've known: the spiritual wars, the napalm and cordite and nuclear wars, and the war against nature. When it was written, the poem "Simple Eyes (Fields)" felt like my most gestural poem, gestural in the sense of the abstract expressionist artists, a part of spiritual autobiography.

There are travel poems in *Simple Eyes;* I had not expected to be in Samburu, north central Kenya, again, and to see prints of gazelle hooves in the talcum-fine brown dust of the road while hearing ravens. It was unexpected to be in Hotel Santa Monica, in California, writing a poem and hearing the old sound of the new traffic as my hair turns white. And now I find that the myriadness of my mind has deepened and that I have a new love and she smiles at me.

My poetry is not written in free verse but in a poetics that Charles Olson called projective verse. Those who have not read my poetry before will discover that I write with a breath line and that I listen to the syllable as it appears in my voice or on the tip of my pen or on my screen or on my field of energies.

Rather than being an untutored or naive form of poetry, projective verse is the most difficult to write; not only is it the most new, it is also capable of including, and sometimes does include, the old shapes of iambs and metric counts and rhymes and near rhymes.

Whether one thinks of Blake, or of Artaud, who used his psychosis as an instrument to explore the realms, or Su Tung-po, who saw his body as a ship upon the river, true poetry is always art. Poetry is not conventional social literature; it is the discovery of the materiality of consciousness, whether in the sound of a car starting, the tension of a shoulder muscle, or the floating of an owl feather in a breeze.

When I speak of things or events I have usually experienced them. It is good fortune to have friends who have shown me eagles and serpentine cliffs and trees flowering with morning glory blossoms. Some of these poems are dedicated to friends, like "Grieved Skull" for Allen Ginsberg and "Moment's Muse" for Norma Schlesinger, and "Haikus" for Harry Hunt and Monika Clark, but they are all for friends such as Pam and Hans Peeters, Richard Felger, Ray and Dorothy Manzarek, Frank Wildman, and Carol and Gary Snyder. But that only begins a list that would be surprisingly long.

My gratitude to the editor of this book, Peter Glassgold, and to the staff of New Directions, and additional praise to J. Laughlin for his half-century of devotion to poetry.

Michael McClure

For Amy

Poetry is a mirror which would make
beautiful that which is distorted.

SPIRIT'S DESPERADO

SPIRIT'S DESPERADO

SPIRIT'S DESPERADO I, I CHEER AND BRAVO
    THE SIDE OF NEGATION AND OF HUNGER
        FOR SOUL.
As a boy I saw the mole
       AND THE EAGLE
soaring and burrowing together
  and imagined that love
    was created of hair and of feather
      that rubbed on the edge
      of
      the
      vast ledge
of Sight, Sound, Taste, Touch—and of the Smell
    of satin and silk, and of the guts
    of the butchered creature
that writhes and grows a brain.
  I was sure that it was not Hell
    that I was living
  but I was reflecting the stain
  of that Huge Being
      called
      THE
      STARS!!

I KNEW IT WAS NOT EVEN HEAVEN

    BUT IT IS ALL-DIVINE!

To be alive is to feast on desperation!

CREAM HIDDEN

Beginning with lines by Rumi

"LIKE CREAM HIDDEN IN THE SOUL OF MILK
no-place keeps coming into place."
No-place is where I am at.
My soil is where no toil
          will upearth it.

What I call *heart* starts breathing
in the full moon
       while the sun goes down
in pink and blue and scarlet.
The mind is just a harlot
looking for some solid thing
     to bet on.
WE GO SO FAR BACK IN SO MANY STREAMERS
        moving through the mindful
        and mindless
shapes of matter,
like colloidal particles of oil
     in milk,
that we pretend that we awake
     and then declare
     that we were dreamers

—and that we know this thing of fin
and hoof and spit and steel
      and that we are not puzzled
        by the surface
          of its
          gleaming!

THE LAST WALTZ

INNOCENT AS THE SMILE OF A COUGAR;
clean as the smile of a snake
  I'm the hand of the squid
I'm the laugh that I hear when I shake
  I'm the sunbeam on the ocean
I'm the monster of life that moves in the waves
   There's a planet of fiends in a nerve cell
and every pebble sings and raves

      I

      AM

      THIS
      THING

      OF

      SPIRIT

that blows up the idea of heaven and hell
   I am the one who shaves off his consciousness
from the heads of old gods
     who drowned in the well

Innocent as the smile of a cougar
clean as the mind of a snake
  I'm the hand of the squid
I'm the laugh that I hear when I shake
  I'm the sunbeam on the ocean
I'm the monster of life that moves in the waves
     There's a planet of fiends in a nerve cell
and every pebble sings and raves

OLD WARHOLS

HOW I LOVE TO LOOK AT OLD WARHOLS.
THE CREEPY SLEAZE of a field of Marilyn's lips
is as sweet as a dark blue electric chair.
I'm moved by the flush of aging yellow hair
etched with patterns of dark shadows
    in which I smell the stench of the subway.
    The "Car Crash" amazes me again and again
    with its childlike delight in the obvious.
These doodled dollar signs are as close as one comes
    to pastoral innocence. Mickey Mouse stares,
    with the big smile and lip-hanging delight
    of a five year old, at the face of someone
    getting a blowjob. The green and blue patinas
    of the puddles of someone's piss
        in a pool on the canvas
                    are gentle and classic
contrasted with what I believe
    is hidden just under the eyelids
of many whom I see in the smoky streets.

There are others that I hear in movie theaters

in high-pitched braying

with their eyes bulged out

like giant pollywogs

as they watch some unspeakable act

wrecking human flesh

and belittling what it means

to be A BEING OF CONSCIOUSNESS.

WRITING TO YOU FROM SEATTLE

THE HUGE CAR SOUNDS
  are dreams in the shapes
  of the thoughts of Mallarmé
  and of seals and icebergs
  and of the elephants and wheels
  that whirl in the snowflakes
    MAKING
      A
    STORM
  that swells
  just over the edge
  of the future.
    I
REMEMBER
    YOUR
soft-fingered hand
as alert as the face
  of a buck
in a world of light,

surrounded

by

darkness,

in

the

headlights.

MEXICAN MOUNTAINS

MEXICO SEEN FROM
THE MOVING CAR

THERE ARE HILLS LIKE SHARKFINS
                    and clods of mud.
The mind drifts through
in the shape of a museum,
in the guise of a museum,
dreaming dead friends:
Jim, Tom, Emmet, Bill.
—Like billboards their huge faces droop
and stretch on the walls,
on the walls of the cliffs out there,
where trees with white trunks
        make plumes on rock ridges.

My mind is fingers holding a pen.

Trees with white trunks
        make plumes on rock ridges.
Rivers of sand are memories.
Memories make movies
        on the dust of the desert.
Hawks with pale bellies
        perch on the cactus,
their bodies are portholes
        to other dimensions.

This might go on forever.

I am a snake and a tiptoe feather
at opposite ends of the scales
as they balance themselves
against each other.
This might go on forever.

Forever is the moment
when nothingness fails.

This might be dust or a river—

"The everlasting universe
                of things
flows through the mind
                and rolls
                its rapid waves,
Now dark—now glittering—
                now reflecting gloom . . ."

THE BUTTERFLY

YELLOW AND BLACK,
   black and yellow . . . in a smooth flicker
the butterfly raises and lowers
her wings,
        in a smooth flicker,
    as she steps
    in an awkward walk
    like a dancer.
    She sips the taste of the mountain
    from the red-black mud,
    from the red-black mud
    near the river.

  The gray-silver clouds are ocelot spots
and a stone peak stares from a notch in green cliffs.

    She sips the taste of the mountain
    from the red-black mud
    and
    a cowbell rings
             in the shadow of clouds.

QUETZALCOATL SONG

QUETZALCOATL, PUT ON YOUR MASK
                    OF TURQUOISE,
paint checkered squares
        of yellow and black
        on your forehead.
Hide your hideous wrinkles
        and sunken red eyes.
Cover yourself with capes of feathers.
Layer your chin in blue feather veils.
    PUT
    ON
    YOUR
    MASK OF TURQUOISE.
Paint your lips with scarlet!

That is not you in the smoking mirror.

Here, this is you in the deep clear pool.
This is you in the music the rattlesnake sings.

That is not you with the thorny skin.
That is not you with the red coal eyes.

You spend the night in an orgy with your sister.

Here, this is you as you dance
        with the hummingbirds
        with their black heads and scarlet wings.

This is you as you walk
        where the deer
        eat the fallen white flowers.

You are the child in your heart,
    grown halfway into a god.

Now you sleep in your stone coffin.

Now you burn yourself and rise in flames.

You are a star in the sky,
      a star in the sky,
    with the murderers of your father.

READING FRANK O'HARA IN
A MEXICAN RAINSTORM

"THE ENORMOUS BLISS of American death,"
is not so huge here, Frank,
where the rain has fallen for twelve hours
into the blue pool
                    in the patio
                    where it rises
nearing the point where it will flood the house.
The sound of the beat on the roof
resembles the dream of a hive of bees.

Somewhere a little boy stands under
        an old tin roof.
There is a postcard of Art Blakey tacked
        to the white plaster wall
and muddy shoes grow warm in front of the fire.

I remember your broken nose, Frank,
and the Gauloise that hangs
                from your mouth.

Somewhere a little boy stands under
        an old tin roof
and he takes off his straw hat
and he scratches his hair.

MIRRORING FLAME IN
THE FIREPLACE

THE FIRE IS LIVID under the log
and it goes out
            then returns
in a lengthening luminous flicker
of an orange the color
of the dazzle of sun
that falls on a forest of cactus
or on willows at the side of a river.

        THEN
          A
        COAL
      FLASHES
         OUT

          in
          a
          big
          purple
          star
          with
          eleven
          points

in a kaboom and a crackle!

It's the mind
in a mirror of flames!

SIMPLE EYES

(FIELDS)

FOREWORD

The kid standing in the vacant lot scratching magic marks in the dirt with a stick, directing the universe of spaceships and angel armies and huge caves and vast beings in their configurations, is the same as the gestural poet who imagines that with his new poem he can discover the origin of matter. We know there is a point where the body comes into being as the simultaneous expression of spirit and matter. In the language of a state of crisis, it is conceivably possible to discover the flaring of a sensory perception into universality, or to touch a point of consciousness where it joins an insight into reality.

You can take the artist out of the child, but you can't take the child out of the artist. The artist is the one who maintains, in some guise or other, the bond of vision-play with his childhood.

The boyhood photograph that first appears in "Fields" begins to change and become another photo from the same years and sometimes the two montage together. The boy in the picture spreads through the fields, and I participate in the gestural act of poetry that is discovering the memories of events of consciousness.

While speaking with a friend I mentioned "spiritual autobiography," as the term is used in American abstract expressionist painting. He recounted what a scholar of Native Americans told him regarding the difficulty of getting autobiographical information from his subjects. They believe that lives are alike and that little is unique about any individual life. When they are pressed further for autobiography they respond by speaking of profound or important dreams and of spiritual happenings. A gestural art uses the material of dreams and spirit understandings along with the universality of the physical gesture that is part of the creation of the work of art. Demands for communication are of small voice when art is pushing towards a oneness with the possibilities of imagination. Of course loss of communication is risked but the goals are high, and as Whitehead said, "It is the business of the future to be dangerous." A safe art looking to an audience for its justification is sometimes a bland thing.

The photo presented in "Fields" was taken in W.W.II. I have lived in that war, and in wars of the ego, and in the Cold War, and in the war against the environment, and in the spiritual war, and in the Korean War, and in the Vietnamese War, and now in another massacre in the Middle East. It is a state of crisis and Mallarmé was right, poetry is the language for it.

FIELD 1

THESE ARE MY FINE SWEET POEMS!! Immortal as butterfly wings
and the song that the eagle sings as he screams
diving! When I stare at all things there
I float in them
locked in the vision.
Still burning through black smoky holes!
Still smelling the stench that I know
is MYSELF BURNING
I am fine and sweet and rebellious
MYSELF BURNING
The Ghost of my Actions
Sexual! Loving! Incomprehensible!
Not knowing the black caves of meat of the self

SINGING!

LAUGHING!!

THIS SOFT VELVETY PURPLE FLOWER IN MY HAND,

I stand on the mountain top

with a startled Owl who flies round my Head!

Even the RED, GRAY AND GREEN LICHENS under my feet
on the scatter of rocks
have histories

The cold sunny smell in the air

and the scent of myself

AS

A

YOUNG

MAN

inform the Future!

Who will doubt that?

—And I DON'T know it!

THIS IS THE PRICE OF THE BLACKNESS AS IT MAKES
ITSELF REAL WITH OWLISH STARE!!!!!!!!

A hand twisting the ear of a dog till it moans.

FIELD 2

AND THIS IS THAT HUGE, THAT new, that instant moment

THAT INSTANT MOMENT
that I read about in skulls I hold
within my hand.
The knobs, the pits, the caves the brain makes
for consciousness of wolves, deer, mice, men.
That can only be a tiny part, a piece, a whit of it.
It all spreads through vision of the flesh

AND

IT SEEMS
that
most of what I know is covert and secret,
lost to me as the green
and shining world of moss, and smell

of childhood friends and classrooms
or the smell of ducks that walk in excrement
by ponds
or the ice castles
where we slipped and fell!!

SO

THERE
ARE

TENDRILS

of every THING, PERCEPTION,
SYNAPTIC FLASH OR MURMUR.
Here is where there is power, that is no power but life.

THIS IS LIFE AS WE'LL NEVER KNOW IT!
SHINING!!

Shining in our lives!!!

Effulgent, beaming, clear as mottled rocks in Streams!
Dew on the gleaming skin of cars. —Fistfuls
   of flowering grass among the garbage cans!

Star systems in these fingernails
are the same as those out there in Space.
      MEAT IS IMAGINATION.

FIELD 3

THE ONLY VISION IS SIGHT-SENSE AND CRIES
           still echoing in meat
    that is the blackness passed. Not muscles there
   not just baby's pleasure and his screams. All metaphors
    of stars and quarks and of matter walls. With tendrils stretching
           FIRST TO LAST
              AND

           LAST
             to
           FIRST

It does not stop with meatly edge or bulk
    or hunk
           nor is it made
    to be a thoughtful bloody splatter of a blast,
        in a little photograph with rounded edges—that is slick
              and sleek un-aged by time.
The kid has a bright red Y stitched upon his sleeveless

                              sweater
    and his chubby fingers hold some leaf or stick or thing
       or leather coin purse
    and he looks down on it
                  and out into eternity
    and past and present that have no edge, no end, and no
       beginning.
   IT IS ALL SO CLEAR! SO CLEAR THAT STARS
           are flesh
   ARE FLESH OF VISIONS.
           Thoughts
           painted
              on
              the

    walls
   of loves and Wars!

Like the smell of damp leaves in rainy ditches
  or flaming auto tires around the neck of victims.

WAY WAY WAY IN THERE IS EVERYTHING OUTSIDE

  Everything outside and its patterns.

  While we prepare to slash the Arab sand with bombs!!!!

FIELD 4

THIS KNOTTED writhing   silver   silky   path I pull
  to raise myself
   twists, contracts, outspreads, stands up
   lies down
     and it is ME
   in all the Blackened Clouds.
My feet grow wet and cold at start of war!
 This copper penny-colored leaf with red, abstract,
and spreading blob laid upon a chartreuse lake

   IS
   THE
   MODEL
  of another thing

 and bodies hurl out unproportioned chunks of weight!
   (Weight of Spirit.
   Weight of Gesture.
   Weight of flesh.)

_____

     Each mind is a Body blown to shit and Bait!

_____

The severed hand (sailing through the air) is a skull of stars
   like the wildflowers on the plain
   AT CRATER'S EDGE

   AT CRATER'S EDGE
  we prey for selves
    in
   cordite stink

and pool of crawling oil

Today, as all days, is day one of War.

> THOUGH
> I
> DESTROY
>
> MYSELF
> I
>
> LOVE THESE MUSCLES
> of my Acts.

"His vision . . . he's looking beyond the war," a general says.

Cute old men look at me from glassy screens.

FIELD 5

AND SO I AM REBELLIOUS AND I'M SINGING
AND MADE
OF BLACK SMOKY HOLES
!!!
These melodies are thought and mete to be themselves.

OH
I
AM
SOMEWHERE
ELSE

but not some other Thing except the flush and flood
of gestured memories.
It is this deep and smells of all things burning
while the nostrils seek for love
that's thin as thought and slabs of lead.

All things droop and hurl themselves,

_____

when seen with simple eyes

WHEN SEEN with simple eyes:

a leaf, a stem, a white-haired man,
a T.V. set, a missile launch,
a haunch of ham. A CONSCIOUSNESS

_____

AND I'M NOT GETTING THERE

((AND THE CLOUD OF MEAT AND MEMORY THAT'S
      in no time at all. That's
    in no time at all. —Blackberry vines
  in storms! And the mothers, fathers, worms,
  and grandpas/grandmas inhabiting all shapes
        AND FORMS
IN THE INITIATING STIR OF QUARKS AND CHARMS
  on the banner of old nothingness
     where all things dance!

    When seen with simple eyes.))

FIELD 6

IT IS DOWN INSIDE BENEATH THE BEAT AND BLAZE.
It is the light of stars
on fields
when seen with simple eyes.
(Upon a face: a copper penny-colored leaf,
a buzz of bees within a leather coin purse,
a blaze of sun on fingerprinted schoolroom glass,
all echoing the screams that started
when this nothingness began.

A
POOL
that organizes life
turns walls to shapes like pollywogs
and morning glories into trees
and desert mud to melting glass.

These tentacles that move
all ways, all times, all senses, all at once
from memories of spots on underwear
to chips in ivory on tusks

ARE   ARE

ALL   ALL

ONE   ONE

thing:

TEN
trillion in-
finities

carved from the shadow
           of Nothingness
  —goes one Old Story!

Still I stand here, still I breathe,
still I shake in fear, still I laugh
    and kiss a lover's eyes
while she holds my hand. I eat and burn
    and crawl
           through Dreams.

I WALK ON MOSS AND CRAWL THROUGH DREAMS.

FIELD 7

RECOVER FROM THE WAR AND FEAST ON DREAMS:
  this is
A SWALLOW'S SHADOW ON A SWINGING DOOR
  and all the weight of triumphs and of tanks
  bursting at their seams.

     GIVE
     THANKS

       to
       self

for each gesture that one makes.

((This cloud of self   is not self nor ego nor what
  it seems. Nor what it seems with simple eyes.
  Not black snails in mud or curling galaxies,
    not atoms peppering on shields
  that draw their shapes from screens
    beyond the edge of any world
         unto

    THIS HAND

    THIS HAND

    THIS HAND

that holds a leaf or twig or piece of gum or chocolate, ice-milk
Whale Bar—with a tiny, red, plastic Pegasus for prize

OUT THERE ARE THE MOUNTAINS!
  just beyond the blue-black waves.

Each wave is as unreal as anything that seems to be
        and beats upon the HAND with froth and sand,

    in these dimensions where friends die
    and cars crash and big macs burn and fry
    in the minds of kids.
    —In there are the mountains!
        just within the blue-black waves.

        THIS HAND
        holds a leather coin purse
            with a honey bee inside
            that makes a buzz

        THIS IMAGINATION smiles
            with thoughts of what can be done

        There are hills with ferns and houses
            just beyond the finger-mottled glass

FIELD 8

AND))) I LIKE THIS SLEEVELESS V NECK GRAY SWEATER.
The wool can't scratch my arms or neck
   and there's a plump red Y of felt
that's stitched on it with a white edge.
The wind blows on my eyes and the sun
    makes me squint. I can't
look at the camera. There's a black
      and pink, flame-orange flash
  and light that hurts the spot I see
     INSIDE   INSIDE
       MY   MY
     HEAD   KNEES AND FEET

   If
   there
   may
   be
   a soul
   it's built
       with simple eyes
     and gestures with a leaf or twig
  or dropping bombs or baby cries.
BUT THERE IS THIS THING I AM YOU ARE WE BE

with taste of chocolate ice-milk in the mouth
   and blood upon the childish thumb.

   Drunken cries and bodies falling on the floor.
     Photon hunks in endless gravity.
    The only light is infant memory
        that's STREAMING
       from our sun

and spraying from the father's lids and brow.

We play in dust in lightless concrete caves
and hurl our gray and hardened clods of mud
            (gray and hardened clods of mud)
               through the clouds of smell
                  rosemary makes.

FIELD 9

THE STATE OF CONSCIOUSNESS THAT'S HERE
IS EVERYWHERE
except it's without senses or with other
ones than these.

Everything out there is inside of me. All that's
here inside, is there.

There is no Blankness on this blankness where
everything is alive

ALIVE
as flocks of robins
in the vale,
twittering on red berry branches
waving in the sky. Helicopters
beating thuds of air.
Streamers of stuff in space
a billion light years, kalpas,
or nanoseconds, hence.

WHILE I HOLD THIS LEAF OR TWIG WITHIN MY HAND.
The wind moves gray wool
I squint my eyes
Red felt absorbs the sun in shape of Y
AND I AM FREE to be these dreams, hormones,
games, gestures, hurls of clodded mud, telephones
bear-claw pastries, my friends, flames
of joy,
vibrant ambitions
and ebullient thrills

and whirls,
with silver lightning bolts of thought;
        and also
        SCREAMING
        DEEPS
          OF
        PAIN,

    and everything caught
        in this clot

        this solid
            smoking whirl!

A

WHEN SEEN WITH SIMPLE EYES
WHEN SEEN WITH GENTLE EYES
WHEN SEEN WITH ANGRY EYES
when seen with eyes from every place
and every splot of spit on concrete steps
and every flatworm and every Raphael and grain
of sand from each possible dimension,
   time and every space

  —I AM ALL THE SAME.

    Genomes sink in wells of mercury.
     Stench of burning sulfur
   clouds the tubes,
proteins grumble into lucid speech

    AND
    THAT

    IS
    ONLY

    here   (this spot)

   where this leaf or twig is in my fingers
reflecting in a faint-red, Y-shaped light.

––––––––––––––––––––––––––––

   THAT IS TOO MUCH!

––––––––––––––––––––––––––––

BUT REAL!

All things are alive, and reels
of unreal fantasy of solid stuff.
          —Or not so!

IT IS NO MASQUERADE!

This is no trap or pit

but Liberty

when seen with simple eyes or angry eyes

B

THE HORSES OF INSTRUCTION
FOUNDER IN THE MARSH OF SMOKE
that is their eyes and brains
WHILE HUNGRY TYGERS
feast on Elves
that carry guns
and march
through sucking walls of Oil
like rocks upon a beach,
like rocks upon a beach,
where floating fir logs bump
at highest tide.

The experience of self is what
all things seek
because it is the deeper breath
they breathe;
and he breathes deep inside the fat
upon his chest
and sometimes he is me
with a memory of bright red Y
on wool, white shirt from Penney's
and the death of Roosevelt that's written
on the mental cloud
in silver lightning bolts
and smell of gasoline.
THE WAR GOES ON
and always is
AND WAS
a part of things!

IT IS MY WAR! MY WAR I BATTLE IN!
    I see the gremlins' faces flapping
    on the pointed flags!

    I smell the fumes
    upon the wind!

    I taste the ice-cream cones.

FIELD 10

SEE HOW IT WORKS IN NO UNIVERSE OF RIGHT
OR WRONG
BUT OF THINGS!
Hold a swallow's fork-tailed shadow on a door
with a leaf or twig where young men force themselves
to stand chin-up to bombs. Flames and insults
fall down around the ears and catch
in the tendrils that we are,
and that

THEY
are too!
It is as bright as mitochondria
that turns to jellied bones
sinking in the sog of mud   AND IT IS ALL THE SAME STUFF
of Mind or Meat or something else
we'll never touch.
I'll never touch.
You'll never know it is the pansy's smell
reflected in the pink and black
of pollen grains the size of boulders
and the shapes
of lovers' dreams.

Matter streams upward

from April,

January, February,

and Continents of Imploded Clouds

comprised of nothing

sensing self,

and dances upon a cripple's back
  with the sound of tearing silk

inside the brains of hummingbirds,

REAL AS A BRICK IN THE RAIN.

Rabbit pellets by the dandelions

            and
            bullets
            falling
            from the sky

FIELD 11

NOW I'M HOLDING IT AGAIN THIS LEAF THIS TWIG
   this shadow of a swallow's tail this wooden door
     and it's the Monster Fraud—Dear Geryon—.
      We fly downward threatened
                             by his venom-dripping
   tail, while we clutch his beaming, shaved
   and shining head, and smell the foul breath
   behind his loving smile. A slight wind
      rustles in my boyish hair
      and my squinted eyes peer,
       I know everything
          I do NOT KNOW
       and Hell's circles spin
           below.

    NO PRIMAL SCENE BUT ALL SEENS
         are unknown
    all sins and deeds and senses
      float
           in something else
    like the smell of drying kelp
    on a black shale beach
           with sea rocks bumped
           by floating logs.

The pride of wood ducks sailing on their images
   in ponds: dark green, stark white, beige,
     dots of red and brown

            SEA
            GULL
            CRIES
        in rustling trees

there behind my head,
    while pieces
    of marines

    RAISE
    FLAGS

    on Iwo Jima

OHHHHHH SAY CAN YOU S E-E-E-E-E-E

                    by the dawn's

FIELD 12

IT IS GERYON WHO COMMANDS MY EYES.
HIS SWEET AND SHINING HEAD'S
  a cock
AND DOWN HE FLIES
       and floats
  with us clutching on his back
   to a lower dock
    of Hell.
The clanging of his pus-y
   armored skin
fills the pollution
 of bad dreams with din
and his cracked old claws
 fly banners of flayed skin.
His huge sweet smile might be
  a grinning door
  FOR TRUCKS.

  The drop
of venom hanging from his stinger tail could
 fill a bomb and it is charged with floating
 mouths and eyes and cries.
 We clutch tight to his sweaty ears
  as he swerves
      in an updraft of groans
made by toadlike things half-buried in the fields
 of mud
    as they are galloped on
  by centaur's hooves.

CALL THIS THING A WONDER—I OUTWARD LOOK!

There's something in my hand. I squint.

Behind is the building, torn down from inside.
  (To be reconstructed.) But now it is black caves
and we play, hurling clods of dried mud. Out-
  side, is the smell of gasoline and West Seattle.

Thrills of hormones. Eyes Aglint! Naked pricks
  and feet! (Hormone puppets!) Triumphs.

                    .

In the beauty of his visage is the deepset glare
  of thugs.

FIELD 13

AND SO BEGIN WITH SIMPLE EYES.

Collective suicide.

The burning body slipping down inside the mind.

The mind expanding out way past the muscles
in the smolder of the consciousness becoming Thing
and
THAT'S
A
MYTH! It even has a Name!

.

Call it: shamrock, belt loop, patching plaster, gun.

.

I am this PHOTOGRAPH. Ophelia saw
all things as beasts or ghosts
and they even have a gun
and move through iridescent oil
in desert sun,
when seen with simple eyes.

ME IS THIS BURST OF CONSCIOUSNESS OF BURSTS
INSIDE OF BURSTS creating bursts of bursts
beyonding bursts of tendril non-bursts
in the nada, zero, nothingness and packhorse
over-scent of some of what I feel.

WHERE AM I?

WHERE ARE YOU?

Is some of us still safe in Somewhere dead?

　Snoozing in a metaphoric Golden State of bliss?

Little clouds of dust puff up from strides
　　　　　　　　　　　　of armored heels.

Black lips of Nowhere blow patchouli candles out.

I feel it all inside my brow bone.

Everything is ever there
　　　　　　　　　that touched and made me.

THE FOAM

IT IS BRAVE TO BE THE FOAM
and sing the foam

IT IS BRAVE TO BE THE FOAM,

not really!

Inside is no place but an infinitude
of places
—positions
becoming everything
in there.

THIS
is
THE FOAM!

LIFE-LIKE STARS,
they too are the foam.

The deer antler fallen on the grass within the yard
is foam

as is the dew that mottles it.

Thousand foot deep clouds of one-celled beings
with shells of silicon and waving pseudopods
in oceans in another time and place
are foam
as are the uplifted peaks of shale they leave behind.
The visions of William Blake in future caves of thought
that are meat and plastic-steel are foam,
—as are Whitehead's luminous dreams
—all foam!

Matter, antimatter, Forces, particles, clods of mud,
      the wind that blows in cypress trees, pools of oil
         on desert floors

THE BOY'S EYES NO LONGER SQUINT, LOOK DOWN,

            and there is nothing in his hand
               nothing in his hand that's everything

         and he stares through squeezed caves
            of blackness
                      at a man's eyes
         that shape a photograph of him
            upon the fields of war and of appetite
   for iridescent foam of nacre-red and green and

         MORTAR
         THUD

      on beaches on a wave-lapped shore

WHERE   HIS   MOTHER/FATHER   SCREAM   AND
SHOUT
and throw each other on the floor

               and

               HE

            HAS
         ! ARISEN !

            ebullient
            from this exuberance

and wears this red Y upon his woolen chest
         for it is his
         —as is the future state.

         THIS IS NOT METAPHOR
              but fact:
the green fir forest just beyond the sleek
and glossy plastic edge; shrews, in their hunt
for crickets, hiding in moon shadows
underneath a rusting ford. Blue-black waves
    beat on hulls of ferries. Light moves
    from one place, or condition, to another!

HE'S THERE NOW AND EVERYWHERE

HE'S THERE NOW AND EVERYWHERE

         as are the covers of detective magazines
         with evil scientists who scalpel-out
         the hearts of large-bosomed virgins
         strapped to beds, then implant
         the pump of chrome that sits upon
             the operating table;
     as is the broken toothpick lying
         in the rain; as are the

              HUGE

              HUGE

              HUGE

     PASSIONS THAT HE FEELS

(shaking in his boy's legs and cock)

—And those are the stuff of stars
that are the flesh of passions that he spins
into this rush of neurons and of popping foam.

These make immortal perfect shapes of the moments
that hold copper-colored leaves or twigs within
                                        their hands,
with each foot upon a war and each arm
and every thought in one.

AN ANIMAL IS A MIND!

—A MIND—AND DOES NOT KNOW WHERE IT STOPS!

—Knows little of bounds or limits or edges.

—Goes on into all times and directions and dimensions.

—KNOWING ONLY THROUGH LIMITS THAT CAN NOT BE
KNOWN!

—IS A BEING OF SHEER SPIRIT!

—IS A BEING OF SHEER SPIRIT!

—IS A BEING OF BOUNDLESS MEAT!

—IS EVERYTHING IN ONE DOT OF THE CONFLAGRATION

IS EVERYTHING IN ONE BARE DOT

EVERYTHING IN ONE BARE DOT OF THE CONFLAGRA-
TION!!

This is war that he is, and melts in

AND
IT

IS
NOT

FOAM.

HE

IS
A

BE-
ING

                AND IT IS NOT WAR,
                   HE IS A MAN
                   !   !

            HE IS AN ANIMAL BEING
                       A
                     MIND

            HE IS AN ANIMAL BEING
                       A
                     MIND

        through the windows of his
             fingers and his eyes   .

BLACK ROWS

GRIEVED SKULL

for Allen Ginsberg

OH GRIEVED CLOWN VISAGE
OF HUMAN SKULL,
with pointed bony dome,
and shadow-deep eye sockets,
black triangle nose
and broken teeth that grin
on nowhere emptiness.
Your weight is like a football
cupped between my palms.
You are so light so modest
and so small,
not large with eyes and ears
and chin
but
solitary
like a blue black swallow
trembling in the wind.

·

WHAT
SER-
PENT

OF
NERVE

slid through the vertebrae
to uncurl in thee
and unflex and open out

into a rumpled butterfly of brain
with forward flapping wings,

wings of crumpled fields and nervous flesh
on which were writ
old loves and dripping hates?

Here are the gates
to smell of excrement within the sty
and strings of lute
and juice of cherry.

You grin but you are not merry.

.

What huge holes there are
to hold the tiny eyes
and I rub my thumbs
in
them
and feel the smoothness
of the socket bones
with
fear

and push my forefinger through
the big round hole in
the underside
and sense my heart twitch
like swallow's wings
as she sits in heavy wind
upon barb wire.

"It's not easy being on your own. . ."

IT'S NOT EASY

being who

YOU
ARE

nobody knows

nobody knows

what huge holes there are to hold the eyes.

.

My finger finds the basal crest inside,
the basal crest inside
the occiput in back
and it is the last divide
of the brain's hemispheres
BACK
HERE

IN
SIDE

where the image of the midnight blue,
and orange breast of bird
is slipped
from the thing with dainty claws
that feel the rust upon barb wire

the rust on wire

and is made to be another part of self
not just a separate living thing.

THIS
IS

THE
FUTURE

in collapse

of yesteryear.

—Goodbye Boney Wednesday,
who can hang a face
on
you?

But still the taste of red black cherries
goes echoing through the hull.

Inside of you are ragged thorns
and thrones and saddles
to hold the hands
of thought.
Outside,
on the yellowed ivory shell
my thumbnail, pressing hard,
can make these scratches

while the swallow peeps somewhere
in chilling wind.

You are the stuff of nowhere in this deepness
and that moves me

while the swallow peeps somewhere

in chilling wind.

EDGE CHUNK
for Willie Dixon

HERE'S A WORD

Ayy. . . Gee. . . Enn. . . Oh. . . Ess. . . Eye. . . Ayy. . .

Spells *Agnosia*
AGNOSIA
LIKE A BIG BLACK ROSE
AGNOSIA IS KNOWING
THROUGH NOT KNOWING
NOT KNOWING
everybody knows
We are the petals and the thorns
We are
THE CLIFF OF MEAT-BLACK
B
A
C
K
in
there
way back in there
&
THE MYSTIC
MEISTER ECKHART
in his night-petaled robe
KNEW GOD
THROUGH NOT KNOWING
(KNOT
NO-
ING)
Everybody knows

we are the muscled black
projecting dark

to put the black on

back on

ALL
THINGS

ON
THE

EDGE
CHUNK

material
reality

smiling in the teeth
of old Despair

I AM NOT A HERO TANK
not with thorns or armor
I AM NOT A HERO TANK
not with armor

slipping way down into
the iridescent pool

where there's

lunchmeat on a platter
thin sliced cold cuts on a platter

Grim
visages
of
clowns
Smell of tallow cooking
in Old McDonald's caves of light

Let's throw the cloud
on them
NOT
see them
for what they
REALLY
are

EDGE
CHUNKS

of
matter

splattered scarlet faces
raining
huge-shouldered heroes

heroes
in

gray suits
with thin red stripes

Blue-blistered
edge chunks
on their knees
with open mouths

EAR
SMASH

AREOPAGITE

there are the "skandas"
and the senses thrash

on
Mars
Hill

where the black guy sees

the
BIG
THING
BEING

BIG
THING
BEING

EDGE
CHUNKS

and
titillating

fingers writhing
on the surfaces

OF
things

soft gray fingers
like the ones of elves

THINGS

silver

black

EDGE
that's made of fingers
speaking to the eyes

Smell of skunk
in rainy
canyons
G
A
R
B
A
G
E
spill
popcorn, soggy boxes
landfill
waving fingers

Death is
beside the point
we're always dead

and

in

EVERY WAY
this flesh is every way alive

Our extinction
IS THE PROOF THAT
WE ARE FLAMES

AND WE ARE NAMES
AND WE ARE DOORS
AND GAMES
AND STORES
AND SANDS
BANNERS
GLANDS
MANNERS
AND WE ARE SLEEP
TAPES
AND CREEP
SHAPES
SNEERS
AND FEARS,

brassieres of blackness
holding breasts of mice
and antelopes
that change to peering
white headed
eagles
perched upon edge chunks
of titillating fingers

where

THE
SINGERS

in the night
are coyote voices

of black and scarlet
ROSES
choiring on the radio that bursts the dawn
WHILE
helicopters
puke
on children
and flash out harsh pools
of circling light

DON'T

TELL

ME

this

IS REAL
because it is the edge chunk
of what I feel!

I HOLD THE BLACK!

YOU, YOU HOLD THE LIGHT

I

SURRENDER

I
AM

A
MYSTIC,
SHOVE THAT TURKEY
UP YOUR
ASS
with the fingered edge chunk
I surrender
I have seen the hay men mowing with
red sun scars on their
necks

I
TREMBLE
in the shambles
(in the brambles)
when my Enemies come to get me!

THIS IS THE NIGHT
and I'm not halfway free
halfway free

(WEAR

THE
SUIT

OF SILK

and whistle
in the graveyard!)

Slinky silk upon the thigh

Where is the state of Crisis?

HEAD
HURTS

Where is the crisis?

SHOULDERS
CLENCH

Where is the state of Crisis?

The beggars are coming to town
some in rags and
some in tags and
some in
VELVET GOWNS

Rattles in the gears
of old cars

SOUL?

Hah!

Thin slice of octopus and candied
kidney

There's
a

BLACK
CAVE

BLACK
CAVE

with a mouth
in there

black cave with a mouth
in there

and
it

LOVES
ME

Looking up at me

EDGE
CHUNK

AGNOSIA

MO
MENT
OF
GRACE

LET'S NOT HIDE IT

HIDE
IT

moment of grace

EDGE
CHUNK

I

COME IN BLACK

ROSES

like some hero's shoulders

MOMENT OF GRACE

ANXIETY?

What about shoe soles? Cigar butts? Spit blobs?
Chinchilla fur. Children laughing?
Plum petals? Oversoul or
concrete wall
written on
by stars
and screams of dying cats?
Can it all be the cave
the cave of meat-black
flooding out,
pouring over everything?

IT
ALL
POURS
like long lean cars
like long lean cars

MUSTANGS

and never moves

VISION QUEST

MOMENTARY GRACE

AREOPAGITE

*

IF I HAD A THOUSAND SENSES
I could tell you
why molecules
are
lies
AND
WHAT
WE
TRULY
ARE
Not quarks or hadrons
or drunken flies
or
RAINDROPS
falling on magnolia leaves
or sheaves
of titillating fingers
clipped from the edge chunks
of the things
we smell
We can say goodbye to Hell
hello to Heaven
and it doesn't even mean
as much as sparrow shit
on the walls of a football stadium

THIS IS THE BEGINNING

This is an act of intelligent despair
A
VISION
QUEST
for momentary grace

Black, I break through, black

This
is
my attack
my surrender
on the edge chunk

which I pour out from my inside
my would-be, my soul-heart
I have spread the moment back
and found a lover there
Black is the color of my true love's hair

Let all the edge chunks in

EDGE CHUNKS
have beat me in the battle
that I battle in
I surrender   I cower   I am a worm
churning in the apple flower
I
BEG
PITY
of the worlds
I
make
in my lusts
for
them

This is our beginning and we're flexing
BICEPS
BICEPS
in the shadow of the end

There's no flow I've built it with my blood!

I
AM
THE CLOUD

I
AM
THE CLOUD

I'm just chicken à la king

I am the cloud of
UN
KNOWING

A. . . G. . . N. . . O. . . S. . . I. . . A. . .

SUMMER HUMMINGBIRD

A
SCARLET HEAD
and long beak
float
in
mist
and
leaves.
THIS
NECTAR
HUNT
!

HOTEL SANTA MONICA
lying on the bed

HEAR THE SILVERY, THIN, GRAY-GREEN ROAR-RUSTLE,
    ROAR-RUSTLE OF THE TRAFFIC
    traffic up Pico
    traffic up Pico Boulevard

   —the roar-rustle—

And I hold the bullet-shaped black pen in,
    pen in
    my hand,
    and I write down
    the roar-rustle
    and the dumb brown sound
    of the machinery
    in the crawl space
    beneath the hotel roof.

    Now there are the ocelot roars
    and the sound scars
    of cars starting
    cars starting
      on the street below.

    There is the candy taste
    of white sugar, vanilla,
    and butter in my mouth
      from the mints
      there on the bureau
    —and I think of the crossed leg bones
      on a pirate's flag.

Underneath my hand
is a blue-gray quilt
with white and peach-colored
anemones.

I brace myself
and turn my head
and there I am in the mirror
with my dark-eyed
dark-eyed
unending
unending stare of intensity
and my hair is nearly white.
    It is almost white.

NOTHING EVER CHANGES

NOTHING EVER ENDS

EVERYTHING GETS DEEPER

with more layers

with more layers

   and a luminous

and fleeting

handshake

between the senses

and the soul.

NOTHING EVER CHANGES

NOTHING EVER ENDS

EVERYTHING GETS DEEPER

EVEN IN THE ROAR-RUSTLE

ROAR-RUSTLE OF THE TRAFFIC

UP PICO

ROAR-RUSTLE OF THE TRAFFIC

UP PICO

UP PICO BOULEVARD

HAIKU OF THE HUNT

ORANGE
EARS
and
tail
of a cat
slith-
er
above
tall
green
grass.

Snap
!

BRAIN DAMAGE—LIES!

SMASH
the
State
your
SOUL
is
in

Grow
teeth

Breathe
deep

Cast away
your tv burgers

and
your
mental motel sleep

Sink
your
S
P
I
R
I
T
toes

as
roots

in
stars

and spaces!

Watch out!!

BRAIN DAMAGE,
lies,
and big biting
jaws
in
the
smog
of
information,
will
bite
your
ass
and
skull

off!

EYES AND EARBROWS ARE YOUR WINGS—!!

GORGEOUSNESS

LOOK AT THE GORGEOUSNESS
of
the
vi
o
lence
in *things*.

See the scarlet
on the blackbird's wings.
There is the geode garbage pile
with its coffee grounds
and rotting strings
of fruit;
here is an old brown bottle
and a dog-chewed boot
lying heaped beside
the greasy curb
where once the yellow
johnny-jump-ups grew.

Now there is the sound
of nearby bullets
in the ear
and
the fear
that's felt when one
sees the photo
of a starving child,
who holds her
wall-eyed,
dying
baby sister,

on page one.

Can
mild self

or
soul

go
dark

in the light
of the morning sun?

INTO WHAT CREVICES
DOES BEAUTY RUN?

TO ROBERT CREELEY (ONE)

THE OLD SCARS come back
        making
        deep
    creases
        in my aging skin
—cuts at the right and left
        of my mouth
            that was torn wide open
            when I was a boy
    on Halloween.

                .

Lying on the bed
on another planet
        I
    dream
of my grandma
and my grandpa.
            I'm
        reading
the tarot
of mincemeat pies
and dazzling black
            A
            G
            O
            N
            Y
            !

Light from the pink tile
    in the bathroom

shows
all these things.

((IT'S
      A
   MOVIE
    ALL
   around
    ME:
past, present, future,
    melted
  in the air.   ))

        .

Grit of carbon on the tongue.
gouges on shining parquet floors.

TO ROBERT CREELEY (TWO)

SO I AM NEVER really free
   of all of that
     but
   all that
   is ME,
 for instance:
   the smell of apricots
     and cherries,
       rooster
      crowings,
   and bad dreams,
THE CAR CRASH,
a baby's buttock flash,
   and the lines
upon my grandma's face
and her thick glasses.
Then there were some
    orange velvet curtains
and some sneaky secret
   sexual joys

  AND ALL THE ENDLESS
  STRUGGLES

  in a battle

  still raging in my head.

  It never goes away.

  I try to push it into play
    BUT
  there's a big mouth eating

through the wall
and voices
from another planet

the planet
where I used to be
before I found
that I could be so free

BUT
ALL
THAT
is ME

and I stand here in a hundred
pairs of shoes.

Chelsea Hotel, N.Y.C., and Oakland Hills

HAIKUS
for Harry and Monika

1) THE
MILKY
WAY
IS
another
shiny
cricket
chirping
while leaves
fall.

2) THE

UNIVERSE

OF

STARS

is
just
another
BABY CRICKET
chirping.

THROUGH THE BARS

PRISONERS OF CHILDHOOD!
    We're all prisoners of childhood
    —standing raging in our statues
       made of tears,
                red-faced and shaking
     with our fears,
             swollen eyed
      in clothing all be-pissed
      and smelling of
           our parents' anger
      and our shit.
           I am outraged
     and fearful to be here
     to be here still,
    still I am
    no better and no worse.

        WE
        all
        stand
        HERE
    in statues made of childhood
    in rooms with tiny windows
    with a movie of the future
    shining through the bars.

    I know I am an eagle!
    I know that we are stars
    not prisoners of childhood
    raging in our tears.

    BUT STILL I wish for big soft hands
        to slip through the veil
          and hold me!

SPONTANEOUS POEM
BEGINNING WITH LINES
FROM THE TAO TE CHING

for Amy

"THE BEGINNING of the universe
is the mother of all things;"
we were always together
and my heart sings.
I was a big horse
with a spotted coat
when you called me
and we rode in a boat
and on a plane
and we were silk
and dirt
sprouting with heather
then we melted
and I saw
through
your toes.

IT
IS
ALWAYS
THE
SAME
STORY

—here I am
in opulent grimness
and grizzled glory

free as a leaf
in the wind!

How I love to sit by you
in the movies
and see the profile of your nose.

SENATE HEARINGS

IT IS ALMOST BEAUTIFUL when fraud and hypocrisy
    reach this peak and become exquisite,
    exquisite in contempt for intelligence.
    With black faces or white faces
        we are always
        this way

        as
        if

        Freud
        and
        Whitehead

    had never been born!
        —As if our most contemptible
    or laughable lies
    are the mountain tops of our aspirations.

We are always this way but these early years
of the nineties make me feel creepy
as if I live in a movie
with spittle-spewing, sneering, sullen,
    snide, plotting figures
from the caricatures of Daumier

        and the nightmares of Goya!

CHRISTMAS IN KENYA

THE CHEETAH

See the face
of a beautiful
  and highly
  intelligent
     child
       in
       the
     profile
of the cheetah.
  SHE
  IS
  BEYOND
  ALL
  GOOD
    and
EVIL
and more like us
than we can ever
imagine.

The black stripes
at the tip of her tail
twitch
and she closes her eyes
as my mother used to do,
with pleasure.

Her three large kittens
nod and grin in the sun.

What is human
is so much more obvious
in beings with tails.

A herd of tiny, brown
and striped gazelles
runs just ahead of the plodding
and grazing column
of wildebeeste.

To think that we are *all* of this,
and it flows through us
in mists of spirit,
while long-clawed larks
whistle their presence.

OLD EYES

SEE THE HYENA'S FACE,
as she stands up
from the pool
of dripping gray mud.

Her face, my face,
and the face
of the old Maasai woman
from
whom
we
buy
the beaded
earrings,
ARE
ALL
THE
SAME.
We are the game
of petroleum cities
and
the ancient
water holes.
It is one alertness
and wisdom
in all eyes.

The old woman's
dark brown
irises
are faded at the edges
to circles
of cloudy blue,

just
as
my eyes
have gained
smoky rims
through the swirling
of lightshows
at the Fillmore
and in the howlings
of airplanes
and autos,

WHILE

SHE

laughed

and listened

to the lion

roaring

at
her cows

from the thorn scrub.

NEAR MOUNT KENYA

"The pain of loving you
Is almost more than I can bear."

Often when I look at you
I feel such love
that it is like grief
and my eyes water
and I remember
my other life
that you will never know
—and
it
is
all right
for
WE
are together.
It is the Winter Solstice
and there is a red crackle
in the fireplace
and Mount Kenya
looms through the window
in the mist;
just as last year,
by a mountain
in Sonora,
on this night,
we sat by a fire.

THE
UNIVERSE
IS
A

GARDEN

of purple morning glories,
and crusty pot holes
the size of elephants
for us to crash in,
and big blue trucks
leaving clouds
of smoke
like the ink of a squid,
and peacocks that scream
on the lawn.

THOUGHTS ON TRAVEL AND ART
for Paul Blackburn

AS I ROAR PAST THEM
the gray slat shacks
are boxes bursting
with rolling whites of the eyes
and big faces with smiles and griefs
          and stubbed bare feet coated
in brown dust and clay:
it
is
a poem by Paul Celan
who survived the holocaust
or a painting
that shows the laughter
in a pool of grease.
  I
  AM
  SO
  PRIVILEGED
that this does not touch me.
Hydrocarbons muck the banana trees.
Bags of plums and baby rabbits
      are held up by hawkers.
Carhorns beep out of nowhere
      in the smoke and the smell of goat shit.

Even Goya was a tourist
      passing through
and Raphael translated
      mothers and children
      into Heavenly pictures

and Bertran de Born, the troubadour knight,
   sang of his pleasure, seeing
        the peasants rushing out of the way
of the fires and the horses.

AT NOON BY THE RED-BROWN RIVER

watching from our car under the trees

MYSELF, a rough agate pebble,
or any star
last night
in the moonlit sky
are all as luminous
and
shining
as
the long-horned
antelope
that rushes into and then out of
the river,
balking and faltering,
while he gets up his nerve
to swim past the crocodiles.

.

Impalas stand
making silhouettes
on the sand bar.

.

There is not much
weight and measure
in the Pleistocene:

nerves

and tendons

and alertness

are the treasure

that one
bestows

on one's
children.

CHRISTMAS MORNING IN SAMBURU

THIS IS ALL AS ORDINARY as consciousness:
   the brown velvet dust on the rut road
    and the lumpy shit of the antelope.
A tree bursts out with red
        roses of sharon
and tiny blue flowers open in the morning
     while a pair of ravens quark
  their black vigor
      from the silhouettes of themselves
 as they glide around
     the rocky escarpment.

     Their nest is safe
     in a hole
        that is as
     ordinary as consciousness
     or as the drops of rain
     that will speckle
     the slow flow of the river
     tonight
     as the sun sets.

     The light
     that we think of as thought
     is just one flicker
     of knowing.

LEAVING THE FAIRVIEW HOTEL

I AM CHECKING OUT of my senses:
    I am sometimes deaf now
  but I was always hard of hearing,
  and now there's the soft wind;
and the tourists' voices; and a hornbill clatters
    in the acacia trees;
and Chopin is being played
    very loud and just
    as he was, when I was a child
    with broken eardrums.
    Now a gypsy guitar
    sings in the hands of a master.
    Hear the wart hogs snort
        outside of the tent
    as I quake with the chills
      and the fever,
    planning a route back to safety
    from a nightmare of computerized battle.
     The accordions
  on a forties radio play
    Swedish folksongs
    and a lion roars
       on Christmas Eve.
In the morning,
    in the cool shadows of mountains,
      the jackals are barking
and speaking and joking,
    —the jackals are barking
and speaking and joking—
and there's the clean rustle
of thorns on the branches
and the whispering of termites
as they work in their caves.

MOMENT'S MUSE

AMERICAN DREAM

LET THE LAWS GO
your Passion
i
s

MUSIC!
Your face is your gut

D
R
E
A
M
I
N
G
:

it's a big black car
it's an airport
it's the stink of explosion
it's the sound of the ocean
on the pink inside
of the seashell.
On the pink inside
of the seashell
it's the whirr of the ocean
it's the smell of the sulphur
it's the light in an airport
it's a big black car
dreaming
Your face is your gut

Music is passion

Let the laws go

Don't lean into the future

Let the laws go

Listen to the laws inside of you

Your passion
is music

You are awake in the swirls
Don't feast on the lies

IT'S AN AMERICAN DREAM!

"Evil is mechanical. . ."

IT'S AN AMERICAN DREAM!

You are awake in the swirls
Don't feast on the lies

COWBOY

YOU   ARE   THE   BARE-CHESTED COWBOY IN THE MOVIE
WHO WHIPS THE NAKED GIRL with silver chains

see her pink nipples quake

while your eyes bulge out

and you die like Schwarzenegger-Hamlet
      on the airless moon
and tracer bullets tear
      your cardboard brain
      and spaceship of styrofoam
                        apart

      What is the ache inside
            that sings that you are nothing
      that you are Captain Nowhere talking big
      and striding over butts of cigarettes
            and buying stacks
                        of cheesy things
            to prove yourself?

            Pictures, vacuum formed,
            and noises made of air

      WHAT

            A

      BUNCH

      OF

CHICKEN SHIT

Somebody owns your pale ass
and his greedy crackpots
　　program the drum machine
　　for which you march.

　You've got a soul out there

YOU'VE GOT A SOUL OUTSIDE TO BUILD
　　and put inside of you

　　otherwise you're just collages
　　of the crap you're told to do

You can get your fill of taking orders
　　the stars and fields of loving eyes
　　are cliffs of consciousness

　　Everything you ever thought you'd feel
　　might be there in cliffs of consciousness
　　　where you can rub your hands
　　　　　　　　　and brush your fur

　　　　　SEND
　　　　　BACK
　　　　　THE
　　　　　HYPE

　　and tell the manufacturers to drink
　　　their smoking oil

　　then use the silver chains
　　　to bind them in their lairs

　　that's one way　　that's just one way
　　　　to be a real outlaw

　　but maybe that's too hard

　　Listen to the jingle of your spurs

MOMENT'S MUSE

for Norma Schlesinger

*Resting in a friend's home in San Francisco, the Cheetah Muse
appears to me and it seems that I am both here and in Kenya at once.*

NOW I AM THIS FIELD OF THOUGHT WITHIN THIS MUSE
    THAT I INHABIT
  and She is the Child within
            her Cheetah's skull that is shaped
    to be a spotted consciousness.
Here I stare into a room that's lit by windows
    in a city where there are trees
      and gardens.
She has dark eyes and rough soft paw pads.
      The parked vans roar around her and the cameras click.
    This is the grasslands of Kenya
      with long-clawed larks singing
    and there is a framed print upon the wall
      of a couple making love beneath a sheet
    in twelve separate pictures.
Always I remind myself to seek
        to make a soul.
My soul is the appearance of the Cheetah's head
      which is divine and much more than life size
        in the air between the beds
          in the center of the room.
I am inside of her as she looks out at me.
    This is her mother-consciousness which
is deep intelligence. The blankness of her field
    of consciousness is not indifference,
      it is complexity. Can I sort this out?
This is not mystical, I know it is not strange
    that she is here. She is my soul in growth.
She is one direction that I am going.

She is

the moment's muse. But there is no weight

upon a moment and I do not weight the moment

except that it is a star for me. She sees

her three babes,

her kittens, there upon the mound of grass, as she sees stars

—with pleasure, but it is not pleasure she identifies

as they lean upon her, piled upon one another.

Give me an act of intelligence and endless galaxies

of stars and plum blossoms fallen

on my hand

so that I can look within and smell the endless blossoms

there in scattered wholes of recollection.

This is not strange.

My inner life is out there, and not inside of me.

I am the thumb print and the thumb and the genealogy

of past and future thumbs

and the patterns and the whorls in mountain pools

and streams.

I am a sexual act inside a cave lit by spotlight

in my imagination with a girl

I loved in bright sunlight while she kneeled

and cars zoomed by

while these drowsy kittens feel the Kenyan breeze

that moves the tip of their thin and longish baby fur.

I am not inside this graceful cheetah head that I watch

but that does not watch me from the center of the room

while the kittens feel the warmth of her milk

in three bellies and they faintly knead the fingers

of their paws, while black spots absorb the sun's

heat more than the yellow-orange ones

and makes a tingling there

AND

IT

GOES
WITH,

IT
ACCOMPANIES,

THE
FAINT

SOUND
OF

FLIES
BUZZING

among the engine sounds
and cameras clicking and the voices
of film hunters and drivers speaking
in the spreading fall of light
that passes
through these windows . . .

RED CAGES

THIS
IS
THE
WAR

OF
BEING

A
BODY

IT
IS
THE
BODY
being
 a
war

this is the war of being a body
this is the war of being a body
it is the body being a war
  and I surrender

AND

I
CEASE

the conflict

and I surrender

AND

    I
CEASE

 the conflict

but the waves do not stop
    but the waves do not stop
  though I am calm
    and quiet

and the waves are fields
  and the fields are a war
and the war is a path
  and the path is smooth
   as the muscles knotted in the war
  of the child's head thrown back

gasping, after the screaming:

"I WANT MY MOTHER"

      WHERE
      THE
      DARK
    SHADOWS
      ARE

WHERE THE SUNSHINE
      IS

where the car starts in the fog
  where the fox barks
  where oil drips over the lip
    of the curb

where the body is thrown fifteen feet
    by the crash of the taxi
    in the night street
    in front of the crumbling hotel

it is the war of being a body
it is the war of being a body
it is the body being a war

    and I surrender

    TO
    THE
    DEEP
    THINGS

    TO
    THE
    DEEP
    THINGS

    WAY BACK IN THERE

AND THERE IS NO END TO THE DEPTH
    THAT THEY COME FROM

THAT IS MY SOUL OUT THERE

THAT IS MY SOUL OUT THERE

    where
    the
    war
is the path of my body

    .

SOME

WHERE

IN

THE

CAVE

OF

A

CLOUD

I

LAUGH

AT THE CIRCUS

at the Red Cages

at the ponies

at the shoes of the clowns

I
AM

MY
BODY

BEING THE WAR

of the Circus

in the cave of the cloud

while the tv blares in the stars
        the mosquito buzzes
the birds' songs are roars

        and I surrender

        to the buzz of mosquitoes
        and the clouds of the stars
        in the war of the circus

        AS
        I
        WALK
        THROUGH
        THE
        BUTTERMILK
        SMELL
        OF
        RHODODENDRONS

        I don't want to be strange
          this is me
        I don't want to be strange
          this is me
        shallow as a small stream
        that trickles
        through the waves
        where the birds and the buildings
        roar
        it is the body being a war
        where the soul feasts
        on all souls

and the children die
in the mortar concussions

  I
WILL

NOT
EAT

THE
MEAT

that is mine
OR THE SOUL
that I grow

in April

I DON'T WANT TO BE STRANGE
this is me

in the war of the waves

of the meat

I surrender
  I
  CEASE

TO
BE

the roar of the war

in the roaring war

of the waves
that is me

and I laugh at the floppy shoes
of the clowns
and the groans of the ponies
hit by the taxis

AND
THE
RED
CAGES

mired in the stream
where the fox barks
at the pictures reflected
in the drip of the oil

I surrender
 I
CEASE

but the waves do not stop
but the waves do not stop
but the waves do not stop
but the waves do not stop
but the waves do not stop
though I am calm and quiet
though I am calm and quiet
  and the waves are fields
  and the fields are a war
  though I am calm and quiet
  as a cricket being a star
    in the roar

BOULDER HILL

SURE, YEAH, THIS IS MINE, THIS IS MY INTERIOR
where dark matters lie as I come to the light
of the setting sun where the boulders stand
where we stop by the dusty path, hand in hand,
and peer where the mating oak moths fly
like ghost silhouettes in the gloaming sky
making patterns
and flights
in the green, spiky leaves.
YOU & I
are the sheaves
of this Something Else
that crawled
and danced
and sang
and spun
till
that ancient thought
called Matter
stood on the toes that it made
and pushed us out,
trembling, scared, hungry, unafraid,
in a twisting mass of gleaming guts
and poetry and silence and listening
and sniffing and snuffing and chatter
AND
WE
WATCH
just this once
in wonder
of dreamy awe
as these moths flatter

the nerves that reach from our eyes
to our brains and our shoulders and fingers

AND
NOW
out of nowhere
we've stepped into
YOUR INTERIOR
as it overlaps
and pours like a stream
in-
to
mine
and we laugh out loud
with pleasure
as our stomachs chill
with primordial fear
at the wide-mouthed, fangy, pink hiss
of the mottled gopher snake
who lies on the crevice in her boulder,
as she hides her fright
of us
with brave aggression.
It is our obsession
to be as entwined
as the atoms
in a molecule
of
DNA
and our souls cross
one another
like chakras where the nerve tubes pass
on the body of the goddess Kundalini.
Look, the small plane, rattling over,
shakes the petals of the mariposa lily
where the stink beetle stands

with his butt in the air.
Soon the salamander will
come out for a stroll
and to enlighten our stare
he'll leave the prints
of his feet and tail in the dust
and his amphibian dreams in the air.

NOTES

"Cream Hidden," page 4. Rumi's lines are from the "Quotron" section of John Clarke's magazine *Intent*.

"The Last Waltz," page 5. Martin Scorcese filmed the final performance of The Band in 1981 and called the documentary *The Last Waltz*. I recited the prolog to *The Canterbury Tales* for the film and meant to go on and recite a poem of my own next, but there was such benign amazement in the auditorium that I stopped with Chaucer. Years later, I wrote this poem "The Last Waltz," which I now perform with Ray Manzarek's piano accompaniment.

"Old Warhols," page 6. The references are to Andy Warhol's paintings and silkscreens: "Marilyn Monroe's Lips," "Blue Electric Chair," "Five Deaths Eleven Times in Orange," "Dollar Signs," "Myths: Mickey Mouse," and one of his piss paintings.

"Mexico Seen from the Moving Car," page 11. This is the first of the poems written on a field trip with botanist Richard Felger, to collect specimens for his book *Trees of Sonora*. This poem first was written on the highway looking at the cliffs and desert floor between Hermosillo and Alamos in the Sonoran coastal desert. The closing lines of the poem are from Shelley's "Mont Blanc."

"The Butterfly," page 13. Composed on a field trip into subtropical hills and canyons.

"Quetzalcoatl Song," page 14. Written in Alamos, Sonora, after reading the tale of Quetzalcoatl from "Legend of the Suns," as retold in *A Guide to Mexican Poetry*, by Irene Nicholson (Minutiae Mexicana Series, 1988).

"Reading Frank O'Hara in a Mexican Rainstorm," page 16. The words beginning this poem are from "Rhapsody" in O'Hara's *Lunch Poems*.

"Mirroring Flame in the Fireplace," page 17. In southern Sonora it is possible to see a forest of twenty-five-foot tall cacti, then turn on a bend in the rutted road and find a small river lined with willows.

"Field 1," page 22. The first stanzas were written to lay out a projective field for self-experience. I'd been thinking of creating a larger gestural poetry and of "spiritual autobiography" and had been considering Francesco Clemente's idea of a self-portrait without a mirror. The poem is written spontaneously. The core image, in this field, is of myself in my early thirties on a peak in Kern County, California. I am holding a purple blue-dick blossom in my hand, and standing on jagged, lichen-covered rocks while a barn owl that I have just startled from its rock burrow circles rapidly around my head in the bright sun.

"Field 2," page 24.

> "The knobs, the pits, the caves the brain makes
> for consciousness of wolves, deer, mice men"

—refers not only to the knobs, pits and caves in the consciousness but also literally to the protuberances and mounds on the surface of the brain. In fact, these make patterns inside the skull as both the brain and skull are shaped by the mental evolution of a creature. In *The Brain in Hominid Evolution,* Philip Tobias presents "casts" made from the interior of fossil skulls in the human lineage. If one looks inside of the skull of a raven or a dolphin or a person, one can sense something of the organ of the creature that had inhabited there where the perceptions are organized. (In *September Blackberries,* in "Written after Finding a Dolphin's Skull," I look through a dolphin skull as if it were an instrument of vision.)

"Field 3," page 26. "THE ONLY VISION SIGHT-SENSE," the line beginning this field, is a quote from my long poem *Dark Brown.*

Now the memory of a boyhood photograph appears for the first time in the fields, it is myself at the age of eleven or so, with the red Y from my YMCA club stitched on my sweater. There is something in my hand. I am squinting at it. The picture was taken in W.W.II. I had not thought of the photo in many years. This field was written on the first day of the Gulf Massacre. The bombings started several hours after the poem was finished.

"Field 4," page 28. The penis like the guts may be an image and a flesh vision; it can writhe, twist, contract, outspread, and so forth, in all the blackened clouds and sunny yards of our consciousness.

This poem was written on the first full day of the Massacre.

The quote, the second line from the end, was spoken by an American general on television and referred to the U.S. president.

"Field 5," page 30. The fifth century B.C. Greek philosopher Herakleitos believed that if all the objects of the universe were turned to smoke, the nostrils could distinguish among them. Guy Davenport translates one Herakleitian fragment: "If everything were smoke, all perception would be by smell." Another fragment states, "The stuff of the psyche is a smoke-like substance of finest particles that gives rise to all other things; its particles are of less mass than any other substance and it is constantly in motion: only movement can know movement."

"Field 6," page 32. Images that are either in, or almost in, the boyhood photograph begin to appear in this field. It could be a leaf or a coin purse in the boy's hand. The boy in the photograph remembers being in a classroom.

Part of discovering how much matter exists in this universe is connected with the recently discovered wall or barrier of stars—before the present this star cliff was beyond our seeing. The large scale structures of space seem, more and more, to resemble the micromorphology of living beings.

In Sonora, Mexico, there are thirty-foot-tall morning glory plants that have evolved woody trunks: these large smooth-barked trees, with whiplike branches, bear morning glory flowers and are visited by hummingbirds. Deer come and eat the fallen blossoms in the morning.

"Field 7," page 34. In *Haiku* (*Volume Two: Spring*), R.H. Blythe presents a haiku by Shoha:

> As the swallow flies to and fro
> It's shadow is cast
> Upon the old door

Blythe's comment is: "The most important thing here is not the swallow but the door. What is perceived is the sublime indifference of the door, intensified by its age; but when this is said, not only this fact disappears but the swallow and its shadow and the old door too. What is seen with the eye is seen; what is seen with the poetical eye is 'overseen,' all the life which springs from the dead material of the bird and door."

"Field 9," page 38. Alfred North Whitehead believed that any point in the universe is the universe experiencing itself.

In *The Function of Reason* Whitehead said: ". . . The higher forms of life are actively engaged in modifying their environment. In the case of mankind this active attack on the environment is the most prominent fact in his existence."

"A" and "B," pages 40 and 42. The "A" and "B" poems are not "Fields." They are the entry of a new and related voice. Remembering the ideas of Robert Duncan I allow the book to be true to itself, and to its own life and movements and statements, and I keep these poems where they appeared in the text.

In "B," "THE HORSES OF INSTRUCTION" and the "HUNGRY TYGERS" are from William Blake's *Proverbs of Hell,* which is found in *The Marriage of Heaven and Hell:* "The tygers of wrath are wiser than the horses of instruction."

Gremlins joined our mythology in W.W.II. They created problems in what should have been perfectly functioning warplanes. They were presented as cartoonish gnomelike beings with long skinny noses and bulging eyes. One of the gas and oil companies put gremlin faces on banners that they then fluttered entertainingly, malevolently, and cheerily on strings above the gas pumps.

I had a paper route in West Seattle, and on the day Roosevelt died I stopped on top of a forested hill and looked in wonder at the six-inch-high headlines announcing *Roosevelt Dies.*

"Field 11," page 46. Geryon is the Monster Fraud in Dante's *Inferno.* Geryon carries Virgil and Dante on his back as he flies in huge circles through the filthy air from the seventh circle of the Inferno to Malebolge. Lawrence Grant White translates Dante's first sight of the Monster:

> And then that loathsome counterfeit of fraud
> Approached, and landed with his head and chest,
> But did not draw his tail up on the brink.
> He had the features of an honest man,
> So mild an aspect bore he from without,
> But all the rest was fashioned like a serpent.
> Two paws he had, all shaggy to the armpits;
> His back and breast and both his scaly sides
> Were patterned with a mass of coils and bucklers.
> Nor Turk nor Tartar ever made a cloth
> So rich in varied color and design,
> Nor were such stuffs laid on Arachne's loom.

I pictured Henry Fuseli's pen-and-ink drawing of a huge, bald, great-jawed Geryon with deepset eyes and frown as he sinkingly descends down the shaft of Hell. Virgil and Dante pose in classical Michelangelian postures on the back of the monster: Virgil gives courage to Dante, who starts back in terror with an upraised arm to protect himself from the threat of Geryon's scorpion tail. "Field 12," page 48. The last line refers to the Fuseli image of Geryon. "Field 13," page 50. This field is dedicated to Jack Kerouac.

Describing Ophelia's madness, King Claudius says:

> . . . Poor Ophelia
> Divided from herself and her fair judgement,
> Without the which we are pictures or mere beasts.

I wrote a short poem about the Gulf War at the same time as the thirteenth "Field":

———

FLYING OVER
FRIENDLY FIRE
FIRE FIGHT
GREAT LUXURY WAR
chubbed-out on
tomahawks
&
BURGERS
F
U
C
K

the poor

!   !

GENERATION OF FOOLS

Smear your whole face
with lipstick
and howl
at the moon

A week or two later, awakening in the night, I wrote a note related to that poem and to the ongoing massacre.

WORDS IN THE NIGHT

SURFBOARDING ON HORSEBACK,
exploding on velvet,
the spirit is a huge thing,
DAINTY
and
HUNGRY
and dancing on tendrils and toes
of eyes, ears and nose
but
you want me to sing
about cutting a man's lips off
or
children turned to charred shit
in concrete bunkers.

"The Foam," page 52. "So the distances are Galatea . . ." said Charles Olson, remembering that the Milky Way is a spray of milk from the breasts of the goddess.

One-celled protozoans, radiolarians, formed exterior skeletons of silica through which they extended their pseudopods, netting for sustenance as they floated in clouds in ancient seas. Ernst Haeckel has done renderings of radiolarian species that are still alive today. The radiolarians existed in such vast numbers that their "skeletons" falling to the floors of the seabeds created horizons of sedimentary rock which are sometimes uplifted in hills or mountains of radiolarian chert: an example is Twin Peaks of San Francisco.

"Grieved Skull," page 59. The quote is from Mick Jagger's singing of the Rolling Stones' song "It's Not Easy."

"Edge Chunk," page 63. *Agnosia* is the practice of knowing through not knowing. It is the method of Dionysius the Areopagite and is also that of the medieval English mystical text *The Cloud of Unknowing. Agnosia* is related to the vision of

Meister Eckhart, who understood that to believe in God is to not know God. "Edge Chunk" is an exploration that exercises the practice of *agnosia* as a means to not knowing. Perhaps blackness is the best window.

The poem is partly spontaneous and partly a reworked meditation that has gone through drafts and versions. It was first performed at the Bottom Line in New York City with Ray Manzarek's piano accompaniment.

On asking Zen abbot Philip Whalen to define *"skandas,"* he replied: "The five skandas are form, feeling, perception, impulses, and consciousness. It's these things which run together and give us the idea of I, the idea of self . . . that I am I. The scholar Edward Conze says, that in order to have any idea of what's real, we have to get those skandas into view; we have to contemplate them and make them real to ourselves and then find out that not any one of them has self, or person, or soul, or own-being, or such stuff as that."

"Spontaneous Poem Beginning with Lines from the Tao Te Ching," page 92. Quote from the *Tao Te Ching,* translated by Gia-fu Feng and Jane English.

"Senate Hearings," page 94. Written during the Senate hearings for Clarence Thomas' Supreme Court nomination.

"The Cheetah," page 97. Composed in the Maasai Mara in an old notebook with blue lines.

"Old Eyes," page 99. After the December thunderstorms, hyenas lie in pools of gray mud by the roadside and stare up at cars when they stop. . . Near the entrance to the lodge we bought earrings from a traditional Maasai woman and went back later to visit with her.

"Near Mount Kenya," page 101. Quote from D. H. Lawrence's lyric "A Young Wife." This poem composed at the Outspan Hotel within view of the mountain.

"Thoughts on Travel and Art," page 103. Dedicated to Paul Blackburn, poet and translator of the troubador poets, among whom Bertran de Born is known for his joy in warfare and bellicosity.

"At Noon by the Red-Brown River," page 105. December 24, 1991.

"Christmas Morning in Samburu," page 107. Samburu is in the North Province of Kenya, a game park of desert forest, rivers, cliffs, and rugged mountains; it resembles parts of New Mexico except with zebra, ostriches, and giraffes.

"Leaving the Fairview Hotel," page 108. Written in Nairobi the night before leaving Kenya.

"American Dream," page 111. The quote is from D. H. Lawrence, from the poem titled "Death Is not Evil, Evil Is Mechanical," from his *Last Poems*.

"Cowboy," page 113. A poem written for performance, to be a companion piece to "High Heels" in *Rebel Lions*.